BRITISH FAMIL[Y]
THE 1950S AND 60S

Anthony Pritchard

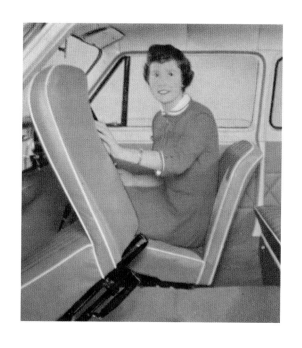

SHIRE PUBLICATIONS

Published in Great Britain in 2015 by Shire Publications Ltd,
PO Box 883, Oxford OX1 9PL, United Kingdom.
PO Box 3985, New York, NY 10185-3983, USA.
E-mail: shire@shirebooks.co.uk · www.shirebooks.co.uk

Every attempt has been made by the Publishers to secure
the appropriate permissions for materials reproduced in
this book. If there has been any oversight we will be happy
to rectify the situation and a written submission should be
made to the Publishers.

A CIP catalogue record for this book is available from the
British Library.

Shire Library no. 489   ·   ISBN-13: 978 0 74780 712 4

Anthony Pritchard has asserted his right under the
Copyright, Designs and Patents Act, 1988, to be identified
as the author of this book.

Designed by Ken Vail Graphic Design, Cambridge, UK
Typeset in Perpetua and Gill Sans.
Printed in China through World Print Ltd.

15 16 17 18   16 15 14 13 12 11 10 9 8

COVER IMAGE
Cover design and photography by Peter Ashley. Front
cover: 1959 Morris Oxford Traveller. Back cover: Riley
badge, collection PA

TITLE PAGE IMAGE
The interior of the Austin A40, from a catalogue offering
six different choices of upholstery colour.

CONTENTS PAGE IMAGE
The dashboard of a Standard Ten, from a publicity
brochure proclaiming the car 'a family favourite'.

ACKNOWLEDGEMENTS
Illustrations are acknowledged as follows:

AC Owners Club, 32 (lower); Ford Motor Company,
pages 10, 11, 13, 14, 38, 40 (upper), 41 (upper and
lower), 42, 49, 50, 51, and 52 (upper); Getty Images,
pages 4, 6, 37, 44, and 52 (lower); Harold Stern, pages 26
and 27; Mary Blathwayt, page 12; Michael and Frances
Grisley, pages 21 (lower) and 25; National Motor Museum
(Beaulieu), pages 32 (upper), 35, 36 (upper), 56, and 60;
Paul Selley, page 20 (lower); Peter Bullous, page 49
(lower); Peter Holmes, page 20 (upper); The Tom March
Collection, pages 9, 15, 18, 34, 36 (lower), 48 (both), 50
(upper), 57, 58, 59, and 60 (lower); Vauxhall Motors,
pages 16, 24, 40 (lower), and 43 (upper and lower).

Shire Publications is supporting the Woodland Trust, the UK's leading woodland conservation charity, by funding the dedication of trees.

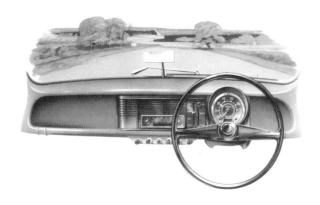

CONTENTS

INTRODUCTION

B EFORE the Second World War, in a hangover from the years of Victorian gentility, even comparatively poor lower-middle-class families kept a young domestic. In the absence of other available employment, she performed servile domestic duties and slept in the attic or the box-room. This class of women grew up during the Second World War, working in munitions factories or on the land and married a soldier, a sailor or airman; very often they served in the military forces themselves.

After the cessation of hostilities these young couples, married or due to be married, had greatly matured and had fairly ambitious ideas about the sort of life they wanted to lead, coloured by what they had experienced and seen in pre-war days. Britain and its allies had won the war and expected certain rewards: decent education for its children, decent state medical facilities (both of which the British deserved and received), but rather more difficult were the house in which to live and the motor car in which to travel.

A massive and urgent house-building programme came some way towards solving the problem, even if much of the housing comprised 'prefabs', prefabricated buildings with a limited life, many of them erected by German prisoners of war and some of them still occupied today. Many people in Britain eventually bought their own house and home ownership is something especially important and very widely practised in Britain – much more so than in much of the rest of Europe.

So far as the motor car was concerned, this had to come fairly low on the list of priorities. The vast majority of new cars were exported under government pressure, in some cases more than 90 per cent of a manufacturer's total production. Steel supplies to individual companies were regulated by their level of exports.

When cars were delivered to a UK buyer he or she was under a covenant not to sell it for two years without government consent. The purpose of this was to prevent profiteering. Second-hand cars were very expensive because of the shortage of new models, but prices eased as availability of new cars

Opposite:
A familiar routine – the cleaning of the family car at the weekend. The car is a 1953 Standard Eight introduced that year, with the very basic specification to achieve a modest price and a competitive position in the market.

Among the most popular road maps in the 1950s were the Esso series maps, priced at 6d, and very clear and easy to read.

improved in the early 1950s. Again, there was initially a prohibition on the import of foreign cars and this was not lifted until the early 1950s.

The alternative was a motorcycle combination – that is, a motorcycle with sidecar – and the finest motorcycle for that purpose was the four-cylinder 1,000cc Ariel Square Four. Most of the larger motorcycle manufacturers built motorcycles for use with a sidecar and in particular the BSA and Norton ranges included twin-cylinder side-valve 'sloggers'. These BSAs and Nortons bore a close resemblance to the motorcycles that these companies had manufactured for the army during the war.

There were of course no motorways after the Second World War, and few dual carriageways; London's A4 Great West Road and A40 Western Avenue were both dual carriageways and notable exceptions. At the weekends, people wanted to get away from home and work, usually to the seaside. Until the 1960s when Lord Beeching accepted the brief to identify unprofitable railways that should be closed, most seaside resorts were well served by rail, but rather inadequately by narrow single-carriageway roads.

At summer weekends, especially bank holidays, these roads became congested to the point of gridlock, and eventually a massive road-building programme that changed the face of Britain for ever had to be implemented.

This included an Act of Parliament authorizing the construction of special roads that were not public rights of way as such and were restricted to motorised traffic – in other words, motorways.

These powers were not used until 1956, when building started on the short and experimental Preston By-Pass completed in 1958, and this later formed a section of the M6. By the time the Preston By-Pass was completed, other stretches of motorway totalling about 80 miles were already under construction. Although the By-Pass was successful, it had to carry far more traffic than anticipated and within six months it had to be closed for reconstruction, including the addition of an extra lane in each direction.

Above: For many years Shell-Mex and BP collaborated on their marketing in the UK and in the 1960s they produced a total of forty-eight 'Shilling Guides', each with 20 pages, including a map of the county in the centre. The pages were numbered so that all 48 formed one volume with consecutive numbering.

Opposite: When the first motorways were opened, many drivers were reluctant to use them, and even when they did, a high percentage of cars – especially pre-war models – broke down. This photograph shows the M1 London to Birmingham motorway (as it was originally) from the Luton spur. The cars are a Vauxhall Velox (on the left) and a Standard Vanguard (on the right).

The initial 60-mile stretch of the M1 opened in 1959, running between the short M10 from St Albans in the South and the somewhat longer M45 to Coventry at the northern end at Watford Gap, where the services became a tourist attraction. It was ludicrous that many British cars proved so unsuitable for motorway conditions – not just 'old bangers' that broke down, but new cars that overheated.

No wonder the Germans and Italians, who had enjoyed the benefit of motorways for so many years, scorned British cars. British and Colonial conditions and even roads in the United States with low speed restrictions did not stress cars in the same way as they were stressed by motorways.

Originally, of course, there were no speed restrictions on motorways. One of the factors that helped bring about the 70 mph speed limit was the testing prior to Le Mans carried out by manufacturers AC Cars with their special 4.7-litre Cobra coupé on the M1 in 1964. In the early hours of the morning, after care had been taken to ensure that the road between two service stations was clear of other traffic, the AC was timed at 181 mph. The story was leaked to the press and resulted in a furore.

Originally, both the AA (Automobile Association) and the Royal Automobile Club (the RAC's rescue service was always separate from the club itself) were not profit-making organisations. In the 1960s members of the Automobile Association were supplied with this badge, the organisation's annual book of garages and hotels, and a key to the AA's own yellow and brown telephone boxes. The RAC had similar blue-painted boxes.

Another piece of legislation that materially affected motoring in Britain was the introduction of the 'MOT' or Ministry of Transport Test, the annual test of lights, steering and brakes for cars ten years old and over that came into force in 1960. It was argued that unroadworthy cars were being bought by impecunious motorists who were not maintaining their cars properly. The collection and preservation of classic cars was in its infancy and there were thousands of old Austins, Morrises and all the other family cars, especially of the 1920s, that were not worth spending cash on to get through the Test and were scrapped. It was a serious loss to motoring history.

One of the first new post-war British cars was the Alec Issigonis-designed Morris Minor. Although it had a quite smooth, modern body, rack-and-pinion steering and torsion bar front suspension, it still used the gutless side-valve pre-war Morris Eight engine. This delightful photograph of an early Minor was taken during a Special Test on a snow-clad Cadwell Park circuit in Lincolnshire during the 1955 RAC British Rally.

THE FIRST POST-WAR FAMILY CARS

B Y 1948 just about every British car manufacturer was back in production. There were 34 different makes on the British market, including the French Citroën, which was assembled at a plant in the UK. The number of makers was fewer, totalling 25, for The Nuffield Organisation built four makes (Morris, MG, Wolseley and Riley); and the Rootes Group made three (Hillman, Humber and Sunbeam-Talbot).

Rolls-Royce also built Bentley cars; the Standard Motor Company built both Standard and Triumph cars. Nuffield, Austin, Ford, Rootes and Vauxhall (the last-named was owned by the American General Motors concern that also owned Opel in Germany) were the leading makers of family cars. Every one of these companies re-introduced their pre-war models with very slight modifications, while development work went ahead on new designs.

Austin was a well-organised if not very adventurous company that built an attractive range of 1930s-style cars ranging from the 8HP to a very fine 16HP model. Its drawback was that the Longbridge works in Birmingham were very old-fashioned. The basic design of the Austin 8HP and 10HP was extremely conservative, with rigid axles front and rear (non-independent suspension) and they had originally appeared in 1939 with side-valve engines and ancestry that dated back to the early 1930s.

The overhead-valve 12HP and 16HP were also very 1930s in concept, with rod-operated brakes, opening windscreen and sliding roof, but the styling was poised and the leather-upholstered interior attractively luxurious. The 16HPs were not for the average family motorist, but were widely used as hire cars and also chauffeur-driven. Austin was run by Leonard (later Sir Leonard) Lord and nothing delighted him more than Austin becoming the dominant company when Austin and Morris later merged.

One of the problems faced by Lord Nuffield's rather unwieldy organisation was that it built too many different models in too many factories. The Riley marque had collapsed in 1938 and been taken over by Nuffield, and it was still a rather distinguished up-market sporting car. The first post-war Morris cars dated back to 1938. The Ten Series M saloon had specification that was well on

Opposite:
This 1949 Ford Anglia is basically a pre-war design with a 933cc side-valve engine and a three-speed gearbox. Four years later the model entered another phase of its production life, when it became the 'Popular', with a 1,172cc side-valve engine, a single wiper and tiny headlamps.

11

Right: This is an immediate post-war Austin 8HP. Both the 8HP and the 10HP had been introduced in 1939 and resumed production after the war, but only the four-door saloons (and not the two-door versions or the tourers) were built after hostilities. They were neat, simple cars that sold well in a car-starved Britain.

the way to dragging Morris into the modern world. The body/chassis was of unit construction and this modern feature was a mixed blessing: unit construction increased the rigidity of the chassis, but it also encouraged corrosion.

Powering the Ten was an overhead-valve 1,140cc engine, also developed for use in the MG Midget sports car. It was an engine of considerable potential and widely used by the racing fraternity with a capacity stretched to around 1,500cc and developed up to 85 bhp. There was a four-speed gearbox. These were attractive little cars, of which nearly 81,000 were built in 1945–8, but very few have survived.

The other Morris was the Eight Series E which, with its 'waterfall' radiator grille and flush 'bug-eye' headlamps, succeeded in looking modern. There was a four-speed gearbox, but the old side-valve 918cc engine developing 29 bhp should have been abandoned long before. There were over 120,000 cars built, but the GPO Morris Eight vans, painted red for postal service and dark green for the telephone business, were rather more attractive.

Another Nuffield subsidiary built Wolseleys, a marque whose origins dated back to 1899. It had been acquired by Sir William Morris (as Lord Nuffield then was) in 1927. By post-war days the smaller Wolseleys were badge-engineered Morris Eights and Tens, with a traditional-looking radiator and the famous illuminated badge first adopted in 1933. These cars sold only in small numbers, and of the bigger saloons the most famous user was the Metropolitan Police.

Daimler made 3,000 of the 1,287cc Lanchester LD10 Ten between 1946 and 1951 and these were bought by elderly motorists who wanted restrained quality. Another important family car of the period was the Hillman Minx, built by the Rootes Group for many years and in early post-war form with 1,185cc side-valve engine and very traditional styling.

Ford had moved to a new plant at Dagenham in Essex in 1932 and there built mainly small family cars with side-valve engines that were specific to the British market. They were exceptionally cheerful little cars, delightful in their modesty, and in the 1930s gave ambition to many who would not be able to afford one until after the Second World War. In 1939 Ford had introduced two new models that were revived after the war and lasted until 1948.

The base model was the 933cc side-valve Anglia EO4A with a very prominent squarish bonnet, usually painted black. It was a simple little car with three-speed gearbox (common to all British Fords at the time), mechanical brakes and six-volt electrics. There were transverse springs front and rear that gave a rather hoppity, slightly erratic ride to match the modest 55 mph maximum speed. The Anglia's senior brother was the 1,172cc E93A Prefect originally announced for the 1939 production year. It was a better-looking car with four doors, but only in post-war form the front wings were redesigned so as to make the headlamps integral and a flatter grille was introduced than in pre-war days.

Ford also built side-valve V8 cars at Dagenham and in 1947 introduced the improved 3,622cc Pilot saloon that lasted until 1951. Pilots were big, solid, heavy cars of mediocre performance and amazing durability, but they were not for the family man. They were more for the commercial traveller who, to be in character, needed to be a big, heavy man wearing a trilby and displaying his braces. It was not until 1951 that the British Ford company introduced its first modern car, and even then it still had a three-speed gearbox.

Singer and Vauxhall – along with Hillman – were fringe manufacturers of family cars. At the end of the 1920s the Singer company was the third largest British manufacturer behind Austin and Morris, but during the 1930s lost its position in the marketplace and nearly tumbled to oblivion. This is usually attributed to the fact that Singer made too many models. But it made too many models because of bad management and a poor marketing strategy.

All Singers had possessed technically attractive single-overhead-camshaft (sohc) engines since the early 1930s and four-speed gearboxes. They lost most trade because many garages would not work on Singer engines because of their perceived complexity, and it is likely that this reason more than any other had caused the company's downfall. In 1938 the company was reorganised; that is, it was rescued by its bankers at a high price.

What's got a choppy ride, a blunt front end and is usually black? The original E04A Ford Anglia. Maximum speed was only a little over 50 mph, but that was good enough in the years following the Second World War and these cars were immensely popular.

The Pilot was a big, prestigious-looking car that combined the pre-war 22 hp Ford chassis, with a more stylish body than its 1930s predecessor and the 30 hp side-valve V8 engine. They would rumble on for almost ever, completely reliable, very thirsty and very comfortable.

In post-war days Singer, like its rivals, re-introduced the pre-war models and from then on it played a very minor coup in the British motor industry. There was one particularly attractive Singer model, the Nine Roadster. It had originated as the Bantam Roadster in 1939 and it survived until 1955, latterly with independent front suspension, and around 4,500 were made.

The Super Ten with an sohc engine developing 36 bhp and floor-mounted remote-control gear-change was Singer's mainstay in early post-war days. The price (in 1948), including purchase tax, was £607 and Singer sold around 10,500. By comparison the Morris Ten cost £432 (de luxe version £444) and sold 81,000.

In the case of the 1,525cc Singer Super Twelve the difference from larger makers was even more pronounced. The price was £768, compared with £422 for a Vauxhall Twelve. Singer saloons had so-called 'suicide-doors': all four were rear-hinged, so if one came open, it encouraged one to fall out. At the time many four-door cars had the doors hung on the central pillars so that the front doors were hinged at the back and the back doors at the front.

During the 1930s Vauxhall produced a range of mainly middle-class cars, but from 1937 onwards introduced smaller cars with torsion bar independent front suspension, hydraulic brakes, and unit construction; on the debit side was the three-speed gearbox, the umbrella-type handbrake that became universal and had a propensity to beat records for corrosion. In post-war days Vauxhall concentrated on revived versions of two other 1939 models. All had a three-speed all-synchromesh gearbox.

They followed a pattern that this factory was to follow for ten years, a smaller-capacity four-cylinder model and a bigger six-cylinder. There were two overhead valve (ohv) four-cylinder HIY models, the 1,203cc Ten-Four and the 1,442cc Twelve-Four (44,000 built). The Ten-Four survived only to 1947. The overhead-valve Type J Fourteen-Six had a 1,781cc six-cylinder engine; 30,500 were built in post-war days.

In 1948 Vauxhall slightly restyled the two models, with a streamlined front end and a projecting boot so that the spare wheel was no longer exposed. The 1,442cc model was typed the LIX and was known as the Wyvern (a fictitious monster shown on the company's badge). The six-cylinder LIP known as the Velox (Latin for 'quick') looked the same as the Wyvern, but it had cream-painted wheels and bumper over-riders.

It also had a 2,276cc (69.5 × 100mm) engine developing 58 bhp at 3,500 rpm, a steering column change, and had lost the synchromesh on bottom gear. The Velox now had a very lively performance that encompassed a maximum speed of 85 mph. There was a strong export market for these cars that were superseded in 1951 after Vauxhall had sold 55,400 Wyverns and just short of 77,000 Velox cars.

Standard had introduced their 8HP model with 1,009cc four-cylinder side-valve engine in 1938. The specification included a three-speed gearbox (four-speed in post-war days), transverse leaf spring independent suspension and Bendix brakes. Between 1938 and 1948 Standard sold 383,000 of these little cars. They also manufactured the 12HP 1,609cc and 14HP 1,766cc

Like most other manufacturers, Singer re-introduced pre-war models as soon as possible after the cessation of hostilities. This company's cars were very well built compared to Austin, Morris and Vauxhall, but much more expensive. Even in 1946, it was obvious that the Singer company faced an immense uphill battle if it was to survive.

This Vauxhall 12/4 was one of the American-inspired range that Vauxhall built from 1937 – with an intermission during the war years – until 1948. This car, which is in Vauxhall's own Heritage Collection, is in fact a 1937 model, but the only differences were that the post-war cars had a horizontally barred grille, plastic on the dash and a projecting boot.

models with side-valve engines from 1945 to 1948. These were quite average cars of no distinction, but they did have leather upholstery and an opening windscreen. Maximum speed was around 70 mph and Standard sold over 22,000 of the post-war versions.

The company was one of the first to introduce a completely new post-war model when Standard's Chief Executive, Sir John Black, implemented his 'one-model' policy in 1948 and introduced the Vanguard. The significance of the name is obvious, but it was also the name of Britain's latest and last battleship launched in 1945. The theory was that producing one model only would reduce production and marketing costs and public interest would be completely and narrowly focused.

Powering the Vanguard was a new 2,088cc (85 × 92 mm) four-cylinder pushrod ohv engine with wet cylinder liners. It was an engine for all purposes and powered the dignified Renown saloon and the Roadster built by Standard under the Triumph name and best known from the *Bergerac* TV series of the 1980s, as well as petrol versions of the Ferguson tractor also built by Standard. An advantage of the wet cylinder liners was that capacity was easily reduced to 1,991cc (83 × 92mm) to fit into the 2-litre class when it was used in the Triumph TR2 sports car.

Other features of the Vanguard were the three-speed all-synchromesh gearbox, coil spring front suspension, hydraulic brakes and a separate chassis. The body, built by Mulliners of Birmingham, who were later taken over by Standard-Triumph, was said to be strongly influenced by the early post-war Plymouth and had a sloping back. The performance was excellent, with a top speed of about 80 mph. Fuel consumption was very good, especially when overdrive became available. Nearly 185,000 of the original model were built.

Left and below:
The Standard
Vanguard,
introduced in
1947, was
completely new
and in Standard's
one-model range it
superseded all the
early post-war
models.
Interestingly, the
prototype had a
1,849cc (80 x
92mm) engine, but
capacity was
increased to
2,088cc before the
model entered
production.
Imperia in Belgium
built the Vanguard
under licence and
their versions
included a
convertible.

Morris's new car appeared in 1948 and was largely the work of Alec Issigonis. For the new car Morris revived the name Minor that had been used by Morris in pre-war days and it still retained (and was spoilt by) the ordinary little 918cc side-valve engine that had powered the early post-war Eight. Issigonis produced a baby car with superlative handling thanks to rack-and-pinion steering and torsion-bar independent front suspension.

The driver's foot-well was hopeless for those with big feet because of the intrusion of the wheel arches, and the headlamps set low either side of the grille gave poor illumination. These cars improved with the passing of the years with raised headlamps dictated by regulations in export territories in 1950 (when a four-door version became available) and following the merger with Austin the 803cc A30 engine from 1953–6. The Vanguard and the Minor were the first of a large number of new British family cars, but they – and many of their successors – were strongly criticised because of lack of innovation.

A NEW ERA

THE CARS built in Coventry and Oxford in the late 1940s and early 1950s were staid in technical terms, but they were what British buyers wanted to see parked on the drive of their suburban semi-detached homes, and were also what appealed in the British Empire. Where British designers lost the plot was in styling, which initially aped unsuitable American designs and later, in the main, was Italian.

Austin introduced its big and luxurious Sheerline and Princess luxury saloons in March 1947. Then, in late 1947, Longbridge announced the first of its cars named after counties. Within less than two years the company had modernised and extended its whole range. The A40 Devon (four-door) and the Dorset (two-door) were very practical family cars, offered in a range of what were intended as cheering pastel colours at a time when the economy was doom and gloom-filled.

One of the best points of the A40 was the lusty pushrod ohv 1,181cc engine developing a claimed 40 bhp at 4,300 rpm. There was coil spring independent front suspension but the original floor-change for the four-speed gearbox was later replaced by a dreadful 'clonkety-bonk' steering column change. The hydro-mechanical brakes were not exactly powerful and the handling was pretty abysmal.

But it was a true family car with a good roomy interior and a maximum speed of 70 mph or so. The style of the body was copied from a 1941 Chevrolet and could have been a lot worse. Austin built 450,000-plus of these cars, including vans and pick-ups, but only about 16,000 were two-door Dorsets. The A70 Hampshire built between 1948 and 1950 had a lengthened A40 chassis with the old Austin 16HP engine. It went well and although the styling was dismal, Austin managed to sell over 35,000.

Austin also built the A90 Atlantic, aimed at the United States market. It flopped. The A90 was offered as a convertible and later as a fixed head with rather bizarre transatlantic styling and the 16HP engine increased to 2,660cc. The Austin-Healey 100 sports car of 1952 onwards with the same lumpy engine was a great success. Austin introduced restyled versions of the A70 (the

Opposite:
The Singer company introduced their bland and boxy SM1500 saloon with 1.5-litre single overhead camshaft engine in 1947.
It was a perfectly adequate and reasonable motor car, but there was absolutely nothing that was exciting or stimulating. The photograph was taken at Bexhill-on-sea.

Austin introduced the 1,181cc four-door Devon in 1948 and sold close to half a million. This, however, is the two-door Dorset, which was far less successful and only 16,000 were built in the Longbridge works. The pedal car is the Austin J40, built alongside a pedal version of the pre-war Austin Seven single-seater, in a factory in Wales set up to employ incapacitated coal miners.

Hereford) in 1950 and the A40 (the Somerset) in 1951. A so-called Sports version of the A40 with an alloy body built by Jensen had also appeared in 1950.

Longbridge completed their range in 1951 with the A30 (also known as the Seven) built with four doors, although a two-door version was added in late 1953 and the Countryman estate car the following year. It was a dinky little car that appealed strongly to the UK public, who thought it was cute and very British. Although it was rather underpowered with Austin's new A-series engine in 803cc form, it was lighter and more economical than the rival Morris Minor, but it still had the less-than-satisfactory hydro-mechanical brakes and its narrow track made it blow about in strong winds.

In 1952 the Nuffield Organisation and the Austin Motor Company merged to form the British Motor Corporation headed by Sir Leonard Lord and dominated by the Austin side of the business, whose power units were to become used by all. Morris had introduced the 1,476cc MO Oxford in 1948, together with the big 2,215cc MS Six with a sohc engine. In 1954 they

The weekend drive to the seaside or the country, together with the picnic, was an important part of family life for many years. This is the four-door version of the Austin A30 and getting in and out of the back was quite difficult. With this family on board performance would have been abysmal. In the background is a Ford Zephyr Series 2.

A very significant development by Austin was the introduction of the A40 in 1958. Technically, it was a roomier A35 with the same 948cc engine and other mechanical components, but the Pininfarina body set new styling standards, and it was both chic and very practical.

replaced these models with platform-styled (flat and relatively curveless) cars of unsurpassed ugliness: the unloved and unwanted Cowley with what was now the A40 1,199cc engine, the 1,489cc Oxford and the 2,639cc Isis (the single-cam engine of the early post-war Isis had been replaced by the BMC C-series pushrod unit).

These Morris models were also unpleasant cars to drive, with, in the case of the Cowley and Oxford, an offset steering column, four-speed steering column change, dreadful body roll and, in the days before seat belts, a front bench seat on which driver and passenger slid from side to side. The Isis in its Mark II form had one redeeming feature: a floor-mounted gear-change to the right of the driver.

The Nuffield Group was very staid and the MO Oxford was a very conservatively syyled car with vaguely American lines and looked rather like a blown-up Minor. It was also sluggish and uninteresting because of the rather gutless 1,476cc side-valve engine.

Austin had still been following their own and slightly superior line of development. The Austin A40 Cambridge had the 1,199cc engine and unit construction. By 1955 the Cambridge was in A50 form with the 1,489cc engine, larger boot and rear window. In total, production of all variants including vans and pick-ups amounted to around 300,000. The Cambridge was a decidedly superior Austin that cornered, steered and braked quite nicely. The A90 Austin Westminster with the BMC C-series 2,639cc engine also appeared in 1954 and lasted in various forms until 1959.

In late 1956 BMC gave both the Minor (which became the Minor 1000) and the A30 (which became the A35) the latest 948cc version of the BMC A-series engine. These cars continued to sell remarkably well. Between 1956 and 1962 BMC sold over 544,000 Minors of all types and a further 303,000 were sold between 1962 and 1971. The Austin A35, which zipped along very well, sold almost 130,000 between 1956 and 1959, but it was outsold by a new Austin model that had appeared in 1958.

This was the Austin A40 styled by Pinin Farina in Italy, with crisp lines and a very spacious interior. The wider track meant an improvement in handling, and in 1962 engine size grew from 948cc to 1,098cc in the Mk II version. Other changes were a slightly longer wheelbase, restyled nose and fully hydraulic brakes. There was also a Countryman version, which was a pioneer hatchback rather than an estate car. You were not supposed to drive an A40 with its tail door open because this allowed exhaust fumes to be sucked into the interior. These were thoroughly attractive little cars and even the build quality was good.

Standard-Triumph marketed the Vanguard in various versions until 1963, but also developed the Eight, which appeared in 1953. It had been decided that the public wanted a very basic little car and the Eight had an 803cc three-

Right and opposite: Standard abandoned their one-model policy very rapidly and introduced the spartan, but very pleasant Eight in 1953. It was followed in 1954 by the Ten, which was a much more civilised car with excellent mechanics, plenty of room and a good performance. They were highly desirable little cars, but failed to sell in the volume expected.

bearing engine developing 26 bhp in a four-door unit construction bodyshell with coil spring independent front suspension. There was no opening boot (access was from behind the rear seats), no front grille, sliding windows, a single windscreen wiper (you bought a second wiper when you could afford it) and basic plastic trim.

The Eight was in production for six years and gradually became more civilised. The Gold Star version that appeared in 1957 (and became the sole model) had winding windows and an opening boot, with overdrive and automatic clutch as optional extras. The company built 136,000 of these rather sweet little cars, but the Ten – advertised as 'the Car for Reliable Happy Family Motoring' – that appeared in 1954 was a much better car. Engine size was up to 948cc and power increased to 33 bhp; the model could be distinguished by its plated grille and it had the better standard of finish that characterised later Eights.

A win, plus third place and team prize in the 1955 RAC International Rally, put the model on the map. There was also the Companion estate car version, together with a van, and the Ten was also sold in small numbers in the United States in 1957–60 as the Triumph Ten (though it was known only internally as a TBE). Total production was 172,500, plus another 43,000 of the Pennant, a rather nasty version with lengthened front and rear wings, hooded headlamps and a two-tone finish, but 37 bhp, remote-control gear-change and better instrumentation. The Pennant survived until 1960, when it was finally superseded by the Triumph Herald.

Looking extremely smart, this is the four-cylinder 1,508cc Vauxhall Wyvern in 1951 form, with the three-bar grille fitted to both it and the six-cylinder Velox and the external sun visor that was very popular at the time. Note the spats (valances) over the rear wheels that trapped muck and moisture and encouraged corrosion.

The Rootes Group run by the Rootes brothers had originated as motor traders, but they had acquired a controlling interest in both Humber and Hillman in 1928. After the collapse of the Sunbeam-Talbot-Darracq Group in 1935, Rootes acquired Sunbeam and Talbot. From 1938 they marketed sporting cars based on Hillman and Humber parts as Sunbeam-Talbots. The name Sunbeam on its own was revived in 1953 for the Alpine sports model and survived on various touring cars until 1976 when Chrysler, who then owned the Group, killed it off. The Rootes Group also acquired the ailing Singer company in 1956.

In the years after the Second World War, Rootes Group cars showed strong American influence in terms of styling and paintwork, but they were very staid and rather unimaginatively British. The group's biggest seller was the Minx, which had been in the Hillman range since 1932. Back in 1939 the latest Minx, typed the Phase I, had appeared with alligator bonnet and unit construction, but it was powered by the 1,185cc side-valve engine that had first been seen in the original 1932 model. There were few changes before the Minx Phase III appeared in 1948 with a platform-style body.

There was still a side-valve engine, now increased in capacity to 1,265cc, and the cars were built in a series of 'phases' until the last side-valve model, the Phase VIIIA of 1955–6. In addition to the saloon, Hillman offered a convertible, an estate car and the rather fanciful Californian with wrap-round rear window and two-tone finish. By the end of 1954 Rootes had built about 120,000 platform-style Minxes – no production figures are available for the first post-war cars. The Phase VIII with an overhead-valve 1,390cc engine had appeared in 1954, alongside production of the old side-valve unit. In 1956 a de luxe form of the Minx became available with two-tone paintwork called the 'Gay Look.'

In 1954 Hillman introduced one of their most useful models, the Husky, a truncated estate car with the wheelbase shortened by 9 inches to 7 feet, the side-valve engine developing a modest 35 bhp. It had very basic trim, low gearing and as usual the handling was much criticised, but it did not really matter as most people drove quite slowly. The Husky had a maximum speed of about 65 mph and the majority of drivers would be content to cruise at 45–50 mph. The Husky sold for a basic £398 (£564 19s. 2d with purchase tax) compared with £540 (£766 2s. 6d purchase tax included) for the Minx Estate.

During 1956 Rootes re-vamped the Minx and gave it a new body with sculptured side panels, a much lower nose and a wrap-round rear window. The engine was now 1,494cc, powerful enough for the Series I Minx, as it was now known, to achieve 70 mph. The worst feature was the retention of a steering column gear-change. With a three-speed gearbox, these were just about tolerable, but with a four-speed box, there was far too much clashing and clattering of the linkage, requiring extravagant movements of hand and elbow.

In all, this version of the Minx passed through seven series and sub-series as small changes in styling and mechanical changes were made; the original choice of 1,390cc and 1,494cc engines became a choice of 1,494cc/1,592cc and then 1,592cc/1,725cc in the final Series VI form that survived until 1967. A floor-mounted gear-change was adopted, front disc brakes were fitted in 1963 and the tail fins that had been introduced in 1959 were deleted in 1964. From 1963 there was an all-synchromesh gearbox, a feature last seen on the Minx in 1938. Just to relate this list of changes emphasises all the nightmares for a spare parts department before computerisation.

Smiths Easidrive automatic transmission became available and was then replaced by a Borg-Warner type. It is only in very recent years that automatic transmission has become acceptable and tolerable on cars of relatively small

The Rootes Group was another company to re-introduce pre-war models after the cessation of hostilities. The early post-war Hillman Minx had first appeared in 1939 and it featured unit construction, an alligator bonnet and an 1,185cc four-cylinder, side-valve engine. The Minx was very roomy compared with most of its rivals.

capacity. There were delays in the gears engaging, nasty jerks when they eventually did, and the transmission simply sapped too much power. Between 1956 and 1967 when the 'sculptured' body style was finally dropped, around 200,000 Minx cars in their various forms were built. It must be remembered that production figures are indicative rather than definitive.

Further versions of the Husky with the new-shape body were built between 1958 and 1965. The styling was a particular improvement on the chunky original Husky, although the two-inch increase in wheelbase was insufficient to improve the choppy handling. The overhead-valve engine made the Husky much more pleasant to drive, especially so with the all-synchromesh gearbox. As with the previous model, there was also a van version known as the Commer Cob.

The same body/chassis unit was used for the new Sunbeam Rapier in two-door coupé form, which had a 1,390cc engine and 80 mph performance. The Rapier, like its Sunbeam-Talbot 90 predecessor, achieved a formidable record of success in rallies. The price was a very modest £695 (£985 14s. 2d with purchase tax).

At the Singer factory, Coventry Road Works in Birmingham, rather odd production methods were used. Most car factories were (and are) long single-storey buildings to house the assembly lines. Singer built their cars vertically from top to bottom in a multi-storey building with the parts being fed in at the top and complete cars being rolled out at the bottom. Throughout the post-war years leading to the company's final demise in 1956, Singer suffered dreadfully.

In 1947 the company introduced the SM1500, which was a much underrated car, only too easy to judge by its bland, slab-sided body. It retained

In 1948 the Rootes Group adopted a rather bland platform-style for the Minx, but the company did produce some very interesting variants. Here husband and wife pose proudly with their new baby and new Hillman Husky, a model which first appeared in 1954. The Husky was a short-wheelbase, cut-price, mini-estate car version of the Minx. Although the handling was criticised, it suited many tastes perfectly.

The Rootes Group constantly made small alterations to the styling of their cars. This is a circa 1961 Singer Gazelle estate car (a Hillman Minx in all but name and a few tiny distinguishing features). This version had a close-ratio floor gear-change and the Group's 1,494cc four-cylinder ohv engine. An Austin A70 Hereford can be seen in the background of this photograph.

the chain-driven sohc engine now in 1,506cc form (with increased 73mm bore and reduced 90mm stroke) to give a very modest 50 bhp, and there was a four-speed gearbox with steering-column change. Coil-spring independent front suspension was coupled with a rigid rear axle and hydraulic brakes.

Singer allowed seating for six people on bench seats front and rear, and the four doors hinged forward at the front and rearward at the rear. Maximum speed was around 70 mph, with sluggish acceleration to match. Because it was new, the SM1500 sold fairly well initially, and some effort was made to update it. In 1951 Singer adopted a short-stroke engine with a capacity of 1,497cc (73 × 89.4mm) and two years later a twin carburettor version became available.

The company's finances prevented it from introducing a completely new model, but in 1954 after 19,000 or so SM1500s had been built, there appeared a version called the Hunter. It was much better-looking with a large radiator grille surmounted by a horse's head mascot, and for the first year of production only it had a glass-fibre bonnet. The Hunter could be bought with a floor-mounted gear-change and twin Solex carburettors.

Sadly, the changes only postponed the inevitable. Singer built a prototype Hunter 75 with a twin-overhead-camshaft engine developing 75 bhp, but it never reached production. In addition, of course, Singer still made the Roadster, now with the 1,506cc engine, and also built a few prototype SMX roadsters with glass-fibre bodies.

When the Rootes Group acquired Singer, the Birmingham factory became the company's spares centre and stocks of the Hunter were cleared in 1956 by a cut-price version, the 'S', stripped of many of the trimmings. Hunter production amounted to only 4,750 cars. Later that year Rootes introduced the first of the Singer Gazelles, based on the Hillman Minx, but

Introduced in 1957, the Wolseley 1500 was a family saloon with a decidedly sporty performance. The low-weight Morris Minor platform coupled with the BMC B-series 1,489cc engine, first-class suspension and steering made it an attractive and very popular model. A version with an old A40 engine as used in the Austin Devon, Somerset and Cambridge of past years was offered exclusively in the Irish Republic.

retaining the original sohc engine which was less economical than the usual Rootes Group power unit. These cars lasted until 1958 and 4,900 were sold. After that the Gazelle was fitted with the Minx ohv engine and most of the model changes paralleled those of the Minx.

In the meanwhile BMC produced two delightful small cars, the Wolseley 1500 and the Riley 1.5, both of which appeared in 1957. These were based on the Morris Minor floor-pan, but with the larger 1,489cc B-Series BMC engine and a close-ratio gearbox. Radiator grille apart, the only significant difference between them was that the Riley had twin SU carburettors. There was also a 1,200cc version of the Wolseley sold only in the Republic of Ireland.

These were very popular little cars, for they were cheap to buy and great fun to drive. In 1963 the Wolseley cost £550 (£665 22s. 11d with purchase tax) and the Riley was priced at £580 (£701 7s. 11d with purchase tax). The Riley was good for 85 mph in standard form and with the permitted modifications was exceptionally successful in its class of British Touring Car racing. Both models remained in production until 1965 and there were 103,000 Wolseleys and slightly fewer than 40,000 Rileys.

Pininfarina's relationship with BMC was following its own misguided destiny. His style spread through the range and the British company's badge-engineering became frenetic. The Italian studio's design for the French Peugeot 404 was much more successful than the saloons for BMC, very angular and boxy, but neat and well-balanced. The first of the Farina designs for BMC was the Wolseley 15-60 that appeared in late 1958 and it was joined early the following year by Austin A60, Morris Oxford V, MG Magnette III and Riley 4/68 versions.

These cars were all powered by the BMC B-series engine in originally 1,489cc, but later 1,622cc form, and distinguished only by different air intake

Just about the only good thing that can be said about the Pininfarina-styled Morris Oxford first seen in Mark V form in 1959 is that it did not look quite as bad as the home-styled model that had preceded it. Pininfarina was a very highly rated design studio and one has a sneaking feeling that the BMC cars looked so bad because proportional measurements got jumbled between the drawings and building the cars in the metal.

grilles, very slight body variations and standards of finish (burr walnut veneer on the Wolseley, Riley and MG). The later cars usually had a two-tone colour finish. They lasted in production until 1969 (in the case of MG until 1968 and Morris to 1971) and of all marques and types production amounted to 866,000, of which the great majority were Austins (425,000) and Morrises (296,000).

Because of the propensity of the unit body/chassis to corrode, few of these cars have survived. From 1959 onwards the future of BMC was balanced between the long-term damage to Austin and Morris caused by the badge-engineering that resulted in a lack of individuality and the technical merits of the front-wheel-cars that started with the Mini and the later 1100s. BMC's messy approach to car development and construction, coupled – later – with very poor build quality, ensured that the company lost its position as number one manufacturer to Ford.

THE OUTSIDERS

Fᴀᴍɪʟʏ ᴄᴀʀs did not have to have four wheels and they could be foreign. There is an important distinction in three-wheelers. Both the most famous three-wheeler, the Morgan, which originated in 1910 and was built in large numbers in the 1930s, and the BSA, had two wheels at the front and a single wheel at the rear. Although they handled far better than all the post-war three-wheelers, seating capacity was limited by the narrowness of the rear of these cars.

One of the pioneers of modern three-wheelers was the four-seater Raleigh Safety Seven with single front wheel, handlebar steering and 742cc vee-twin engine. It was made from 1933 to 1936 only, but the designer T. L. Williams bought the manufacturing rights and founded the Reliant Motor Company at Tamworth in Staffordshire. Originally the company made only vans and from 1939 these were powered by Reliant's version of the Austin Seven 747cc side-valve engine. It was not until 1952 that the first private car, the Regal, appeared and it was a neat, chunky vehicle with alloy body on wood frame, proper steering, seating for four and a maximum speed of 55–60 mph.

A four-speed and reverse gearbox was in unit with the engine and the rear wheels were driven through an open prop-shaft. From 1956 the body was glass-fibre and from 1963 Reliant used their own 600cc ohv four-cylinder alloy engine. In 1954 the price was £381 3s. 9d (including purchase tax) and as a Ford Popular including purchase tax cost £390 14s. 2d, superficially, the appeal of the Regal was limited. In fact the cars attracted an enthusiastic following of people who wanted to be different; the road tax was the same as for a motorcycle combination and they could be driven on a motorcycle licence. The Regal and its successors, the Rialto and Robin, flourished for many years.

There were many makes of economy three-wheelers and imported bubble-cars on the market, especially during the 1950s, and they were given a boost by fuel rationing introduced in late 1956 because of the Suez crisis. An exceptionally long-lived make was the Bond designed by Lawrie Bond, a prolific designer of motorcycles and rather eccentric cars.

Opposite:
It is hard to believe now that in the 1950s the Volkswagen Beetle appealed only to a small range of people. Dealers were enthusiasts, but the majority of would-be buyers believed, like Enzo Ferrari, that the horse should pull the cart. The marque was also tainted by its origins in Nazi Germany.

Right: Production of the Reliant Regal did not get under way until 1953 when the first open version sold in limited numbers. All the early cars had the Austin Seven 747cc side-valve engine built under licence, but the company based at Tamworth adopted its own all-alloy four-cylinder ohv engine in 1962. This is a 1962 model with Reliant's own engine and rust-proof glass-fibre body that incorporated a reverse-angle rear window rather like that of the Ford 105E Anglia.

The Bond started life in 1948 with a 125cc Villiers two-stroke engine and two seats and grew up with items such as reverse gear, 246cc engine, four seats (from 1954) and dummy front wings concealing a single front wheel. By 1966 production amounted to close to 25,000 vehicles. In 1965 the makers, Sharp's Commercials Limited in Preston, Lancashire introduced the 875 with detuned Hillman Imp engine. It was lethal even in detuned form, but Reliant bought the company in 1969 and after 1970 the only Bond still built at Tamworth was the Bug, a rather peculiar sporty three wheeler.

AC Cars of Thames Ditton built the beautiful Ace sports cars from 1954 onwards, but they made much of their money by building three-wheel motorised invalid carriages for the government. With experience of this technique (there was little technology involved) AC launched the Petite with single front wheel in 1952 and it lasted through to 1958. It was an

Right: At the wheel of this AC Petite is Joan Bailey, wife of Ernie Bailey who ran the Buckland Motor Body Company in Buntingford in Hertfordshire. The company was closely associated with AC Cars and built some of the bodies, including probably bodies for the AC Petite.

unattractive little contraption with a steel chassis and body frame with alloy panels and a 346cc Villiers two-stroke engine mounted at the rear. This was folly because it limited seating to a single bench seat with accommodation for two adults and nowhere for the child or children to go except squeezed in with them. It is not known how many Petites were built, but there were always plenty of unsold examples at the factory.

It is astonishing that Sharp's Commercials Limited, a small company in Preston, Lancashire, built nearly 25,000 of these cars over an 18-year period. They still do have a very enthusiastic following. This is a 1959 version known as the Mk C and fitted with a Villiers 250cc two-stroke engine.

The only foreign manufacturer to make a serious impression on the British motoring scene was Volkswagen. Everyone knows about VWs these days, so there is not much to be said about the original 'Beetle' save that it was basic, tough and very reliable. Although rear engines are now out of favour, the VW of the 1950s handled better than much of the front engine/rear drive British opposition – but that all changed of course with the appearance of the Mini. Air-cooled cars like the VW are inevitably noisy, but it had advantages, for motorists were always worried in those days whether they had enough anti-freeze in their water-cooled jalopies.

Right: In the 1950s the Volkswagen Beetle was regarded as a rather idiosyncratic, rather specialist car that appealed only to a rather small range of people. The majority of would-be buyers believed that a real car's engine was in the front.

Bottom: During the late 1950s there were many attempts to market in Britain what we would now call 'microcars', but the appearance of the Mini, and other very much more practical four-wheel cars soon brought about their demise. The Frisky was was built between 1957 and 1961 in both three-wheel and four-wheel form by a number of different manufacturers, including engine builders Henry Meadows. It is not known how many were built, but it certainly was not very many.

As for other imported cars, they tended to be present only in small numbers. Yet especially interesting was another German make, DKW whose cars were powered by three-cylinder two-stroke 896cc engines. They represented a successful pre-war design, updated with neat and shapely styling. Transmission was by an all-synchromesh four-speed gearbox and there was a free-wheel. They came on to the British market in 1953 and once again they handled superbly, but were high-priced and of interest only to a small sector of the market.

The early post-war, rear-engined, water-cooled Renault 750 was a modest seller, but the very pretty 845cc Dauphine introduced by the same maker in 1956 was a world success, with over two million sold, although UK dealers only shifted a small number. Those who never drove a Dauphine only too readily criticised their handling. Yes, they over-steered, but they were very controllable and, also, very economical.

In early post-war days Citroën had an assembly plant on the Slough Trading Estate (latterly used for the production of Mars bars, Galaxy chocolate and the like) and the 2CV with 375cc engine (425cc from 1954) was built there from 1953 to 1959. Afterwards 2CVs were not imported until the 1970s. They always were – and still are – cult vehicles, and their qualities are not fully appreciated by the majority of British drivers. Most cannot even change gear on a 2CV, which has a weird gear-change layout.

This photograph shows one of the best small family saloons of the 1950s, the DKW Sonderklasse with front-wheel-drive, a three-cylinder two-stroke engine, excellent, safe and predictable handling and a fine performance. In Britain they were simply too quirky in design and far too expensive to take a significant share of the market.

Right: Although the Renault 750 was designed in France, Volkswagen designer Professor Ferdinand, who was being held captive in France, helped with development of the concept. These cars sold well in France, but the 750 was not well received on the British market. The combination of rear engine and water-cooling was not appealing and the interior was very cramped. This is a 1955 example and within a year the brilliantly styled, larger-capacity 845cc Dauphine had appeared. It was a much better car in every respect and two million were sold, twice the production run of the 750.

Fiat had enjoyed a traditional popularity with its two-seater 500 Topolino, and this continued in a limited fashion with the 600, a genuine four-seater, that survived in various forms until 1969. A Nuova 500 with a rear-mounted air-cooled twin-cylinder engine (originally 479cc, soon increased to 499cc) appeared in 1957 and lasted through to 1970. They were rather noisy, but had superb roadholding and with four people on board the 55 mph cruising sank to around 35 mph. Not many were sold in Britain.

The Fiat 1100 of 1953 onwards was another model that was not particularly popular. Boxy and chunky in appearance with an additional 'Cyclops' spot light in the grille, the 1100 was a poor man's Ferrari for the family motorist with sporting tastes – but it was much more reliable than a Ferrari. The TV (Turismo Veloce) with twin carburettors was good for 85 mph, cruised at 70 mph and handled superbly. They rotted pretty badly, but so did everything but the Volkswagen, and there was a rather

Left: The Fiat company was famed for the 500 Topolino and the theme of small-capacity cars of great economy and with a surprising amount of space for the driver and passengers was continued in the 1950s. This is a 600, early versions of which from 1955–60 had a 633cc engine while those made later, up until 1969, were fitted with a 767cc unit. This is the SEAT version that was built under licence in Spain.

The 'Nuova' 500 appeared in 1957 with twin-cylinder 479cc engine, later increased in size to 499cc. Obviously, there was not much in the way of performance and like all Fiats, the 500 suffered from galloping body rot, but handled very nicely. They are perhaps best described as 'cute', although there was room for the driver and three passengers (two passengers when luggage was carried).

cumbersome handbrake operating on the transmission. Of course, they were also rather expensive, and in 1956 a TV cost £750 basic (£1,063 12s. 6d including import duty and purchase tax).

Cars from the European mainland were technically much more sophisticated than their British counterparts, and although at one time it seemed as if VW would dominate the market for family cars, it never happened. The take-over came from the East in the form of the Japanese Datsun and Toyota. They were dull, boring, unsophisticated cars, but build-quality and reliability was very high, and that was what British buyers wanted more than anything else.

FORD: FAVOURITES
OF THE FIFTIES

FOR SOME YEARS following the Second World War, Ford seemed reluctant to update their designs and the company plodded along with side-valve engines and pre-war body shapes. The V8 Pilot was the first of the old-type cars to go and it was replaced by two new models that appeared in 1950–1. The first of these was the Consul with its 1,508cc four-cylinder engine, but it was an overhead-valve unit, with unit construction and MacPherson strut-type independent front suspension.

It was a very spacious car and could carry six people on the front and rear bench-type seats. On the debit side there was only a three-speed gearbox with a steering column change. Abbott of Farnham carried out estate car conversions on both Consul and the larger-capacity Zephyr. In 1954 the price of the Consul was a very modest £470 plus £196 19s. 2d. Over a six-year period, Ford sold more than 225,000 of these cars.

The Zephyr, which appeared in 1951, was a much more attractive proposition, albeit with the downside of greater running costs. There was a six-cylinder 2,262cc engine that gave 80 mph-plus in standard form and the handling was reasonable, if not superlative. They were very tough cars, as exemplified by Sydney Allard who finished the 1955 RAC Rally after half-demolishing his Zephyr against a wall. Ford sold 148,000 of these cars over a five-year period. They added the more luxurious and more expensive Zodiac with higher-compression engine, two-tone paintwork and whitewall tyres in 1954.

The same year Vauxhall, another American-owned company, updated the Wyvern and Velox with longer, wider, roomier bodywork. In 1952 both models were fitted with new shorter-stroke engines and Vauxhall's answer to the Zodiac, the Cresta, appeared in 1954. The two-tone paintwork on the Cresta was lurid and the build-quality of these cars steadily deteriorated. By the time these models had been superseded in 1957 Luton had turned out 108,000 Wyverns, 235,000 Velox and 166,000 Crestas. These were the main competitors to the bigger Fords and so are described here.

Stubbornly, Ford retained side-valve engines for their small cars, even though the range was transformed in 1953. The new 100E two-door Anglia

Opposite:
Dagenham was the home of conservative cars, and both these models introduced in 1953 had sluggish, uneconomical side-valve engines. In front is the Anglia 100E and behind it the four-door Prefect 100E. They survived in production until 1959.

39

Ford did not eschew side valves until 1951 when the Consul and Zephyr appeared. The Consul was the ultimate in bland styling, although it handled reasonably well because of the MacPherson strut-type independent front suspension. The worst feature was the three-speed gearbox with steering column gear-change.

and four-door Prefect featured platform styling, unit construction, hydraulic brakes – and 1,172cc side-valve engines. There was also a van and this was joined by the Escort and Squire estate car versions in 1955. The Squire mimicked American 'woody' Fords by having wooden strakes on its sides. Ford's small-car philosophy was very different from that of Austin and Morris.

In 1953 Ford revised the old 'sit up and beg' Anglia (see p.10) as the very basic, cut-price Popular with few instruments, minute headlamps, a single wiper and a maximum speed of about 50 mph, coupled with heavy fuel consumption. The basic price of the Popular was only £275 (£390 14s. 2d with purchase tax), which shook other car makers and motorcycle manufacturers. As mentioned previously, it was only marginally dearer than the Reliant Regal, but the biggest competitor to the cheap car was the motorcycle combination.

In 1955 a 600cc side-valve motorcycle and side-car cost £270–£300 new

Opposite top: Although the Zephyr was a similar concept to the Consul, it was a much better car in almost every respect. With a 2,262cc six-cylinder engine that pumped out 68 bhp, it was good for over 80 mph and was toughly built. Again, the three-speed gearbox was the main drawback, but it was a nicer car than the rival products from Vauxhall and BMC. Both models were available with drophead bodies by Carbodies and they were especially attractive in this form.

Above: In the mid-1950s Vauxhall build-quality was abysmal and it seems remarkable that there are any survivors. After 1951 very few changes were made to the Velox except for cosmetic detail. Compared with the contemporary Cresta that had very similar styling, the Velox was more restrained. This photograph was taken in Hemel Hempstead New Town.

and although the financial gap between this and the Popular was too great for many would-be buyers, what it did was to encourage the motorcyclist to buy a second-hand car. It was the Ford Popular that revolutionised attitudes in Britain, albeit indirectly. Between 1953 and 1959 Ford built 155,000 Populars, 346,000 'new' Anglias (more than small car production by either Austin or Morris), 101,000 Prefects and 50,000 Escorts and Squires. Although they are now a very rare sight, the small Fords dominated their sector of the market.

Ford introduced improved versions of the bigger models in 1956 and these had a longer wheelbase, bigger engines and better weight distribution, but the handling was still not good enough for fast driving and quite a number of serious Zephyr drivers motored with a concrete weight in the boot to maintain adhesion under fairly hard cornering. The Consul II now had an engine of 1,703cc, while the Zephyr II and Zodiac II had 2,553cc engines developing over 80 bhp and giving a maximum speed of about 90 mph. The cars built from 1959 onwards had a lower roofline.

The latest big Fords were also available in estate car and convertible forms. This range lasted for six years and during that time Ford built a total of 682,000 of all types of these cars. Although BMC (which became British Motor Holdings after its merger with Jaguar in 1966) was Britain's biggest car manufacturer, Ford was by then much bigger than either Austin or Morris if they are regarded as separate units.

Vauxhall remained Ford's closest competitor and in 1957 they introduced new models. The new Victor F with the 1,508cc engine was the warthog of the motoring world with styling that was a dreadful parody of the 1955 Chevrolet. It was all lumps and bumps, with what has been described as a dog's leg

Below: The new Anglia and Prefect represented a confusion of concepts: modern, boxy lines and unit construction were combined with a (redesigned) side-valve engine and three-speed gearbox. Even so, they were exceptionally successful and their ride, braking and steering were vastly superior to that of their predecessors. This is the 100E Prefect, which was really a little too short in the wheelbase for four doors.

In 1956 Ford replaced all three versions of the bigger cars, which now had a longer wheelbase and restyled body. A further change was made in 1959 when the roof-line was lowered. In Zodiac form, as seen here, with two-tone paintwork they were very handsome cars.

windscreen, 13-inch wheels that spoilt any sense of proportion and, on the early cars, exhausts that emerged through the rear bumper and were conducive to corrosion. On the credit side it had a hydraulic clutch and synchromesh on the bottom gear of the three-speed box. It survived until 1961, with slight modifications.

Demand for cars was still very high and buyers were less discriminating in later years, but even so it is remarkable that Vauxhall managed to sell close to 400,000 of this model. The new Victor FB that appeared in 1961 had much more restrained styling and it was the first Vauxhall without bonnet flutes since this feature was adopted on the 1913 Prince Henry model. Variations of this tolerably well-styled car survived in production to 1967. There are few survivors, for although the engines lasted pretty well for ever, the bodies rotted swiftly from the moment they first sat on the proud owner's drive.

In 1957 Vauxhall had also introduced new PA Velox and Cresta models with the 2,262cc engine. The wheelbase was increased, there was an all-synchromesh three-speed gearbox and, once again, very American styling. The styling was better than that of the Victor, though the overall impression was of a rather garish, low and wide car. Again, there was a dog's leg windscreen, tail-fins and a rather peculiar three-panel rear window (this last feature disappeared in 1960). An incredibly ugly estate car version was added in 1959 and the following year there was a new 2,651cc engine with 'square' (82.55 × 82.55mm) dimensions and wedge-shaped combustion chambers.

There were now larger wheels and bigger tail-fins, together with lower-geared steering. Disc brakes on the front wheels became optional, as did overdrive and Hydramatic automatic transmission. Production ceased in 1962 after 172,000 had been built and annual production of Vauxhalls was now much lower than that of the comparable Fords. Vauxhalls seemed very

Left: Inspired by the styling of the 1955 Chevrolet, the 1957 Victor F was atrocious in looks and little better in performance. The familiar Vauxhall flutes were still there, but they were on the sides of the body and with all the lumps and bumps, the 'dog-leg' windscreen and, on the early cars, the exhausts poking through the rear bumper, it must qualify as one of the worst-styled cars of the 1950s. Enthusiasts would, however, extol its character and individuality.

undesirable cars in their day, but they did drive well, probably better than the rival Ford and they are distinctive period pieces that have become very collectable. What replaced them in 1962 were the PB series Velox and Cresta, with large, bland restyled bodies.

For 1965 the engine size was increased to 3,294cc and a four-speed floor gear-change became optional. So did two-speed Powerglide automatic transmission, which was fine on a big Pontiac or the like, but not really suitable for the Velox and Cresta. In manual form with the four-speed gearbox they were much-improved cars, excellent relaxed cruisers and even the roadholding was not too bad. Production ceased in 1965 by which time 87,000 had been built.

Left: The Cresta PA of 1957 onwards was wide, low and thoroughly American in concept. Typically American were the tail-fins, the 'dog-leg' windscreen as on the contemporary Victor and the two-tone colour finish. The three-panel rear window was just plain odd. The bizarre range of colours included pink and white. Quite a number of these cars have survived and they have a strong and enthusiastic following.

TRIUMPH
ROVER
RENAULT
WOLSELEY
MORRIS
BMC
QUALITY FIRST ALL THROUGH
MINI'S GO HYDROLASTIC

MAJOR ADVANCES

THE YEAR 1959 was a turning point in the British motor industry. Three new designs that were to transform the motor industry appeared, and one of these was the most important Ford model announced in the UK since the Second World War; it was to lead to the eclipse of the British Motor Corporation by the popularity of Ford's technically very basic but exceptionally popular overhead-valve family saloons.

In April 1959 Standard-Triumph announced their new Herald, marketed under the Triumph name, and the company's policy was to use this marque name for all new models. The Herald in its original form used the Standard Ten engine developing 38 bhp and gearbox in a separate backbone-type chassis, with independent suspension front and rear (coil springs and wishbones at the front, but rather unsatisfactory swing-axles at the rear) and rack-and-pinion steering. The body – available in two-door four-seater saloon and two-plus-two coupe and drophead forms – was designed by Giovanni Michelotti in Italy and was a very distinctive, rather chunky style built up from separate panels.

The motor industry had increased its production potential, but this was not matched by the body builders, most of whom were independent companies. The Standard-Triumph directors were paranoid about body supplies and this is reflected in the body of the Herald, which if need be could be spread between several factories. One of the more remarkable features of the design was the claimed turning circle of 25 feet but, in the writer's experience, this was not a true figure – although there is no doubt that the turning circle was very tight. The price was £495 (£702 7s. 6d with purchase tax) for the saloon, and the other versions were slightly more expensive.

A twin-carburettor 45 bhp version became available in September 1959, but even so the Herald was underpowered. Although the 948cc saloon remained available until 1964, a rather more satisfactory 1,147cc model was introduced in 1961 and an estate car was added to the range. This bigger-engined model was listed until 1967, becoming available as the de luxe Herald 12/50 in 1963. It was replaced by the 1,296cc 13/60 in 1967 and this

Opposite:
From the late 1950s to the early 1960s the British motor industry boomed. The British Motor Corporation and Ford battled for market domination, while both Standard-Triumph and Vauxhall struggled to increase their share. This photograph shows a very busy Earls Court, scene of the British Motor Industry annual motor show, and seems to have been taken in 1964, the year that Hydrolastic suspension was introduced on the Mini.

Both: The styling of the Triumph Herald was the work of Italian stylist Giovanni Michelotti, but it was probably not one of his more successful efforts. Generally, the car looked too chunky, although its method of construction with separate chassis and individual body panels was extremely practical.

DO MEN DRIVE BETTER THAN WOMEN?
— not in the Triumph Herald!

Do men drive better than women? Not in the Triumph Herald. It's the masculine car that delights women. They can take their corners with greater confidence because the independent suspension holds the car firmly on the road. They can master the most difficult manœuvre because the Triumph Herald will turn so readily and visibility is so good. They can drive well because they drive comfortably; the seats can be adjusted in so many different ways that a really relaxed driving position is assured. There's plenty of space for feminine nick-nacks, pockets, trays, parcel-shelf, cubby box, coat-hangers and a big sensible boot — all are provided. And there's even a vanity mirror behind the passenger's sun-visor. Yes, women achieve a new equality with men when they drive a Triumph Herald.

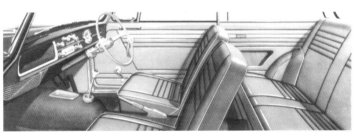

survived until 1971. Total production of the Herald and its variants amounted to 485,000, so by any standard the model was a great success. Another development of the Herald was the Vitesse, powered by a six-cylinder, small-bore engine from the Vanguard Six introduced in 1960.

Between 1966 and 1971 the company built Vitesses with 1,998cc engines. The Vitesse was a very quick motor car, but the combination of the heavier engine and swing-axle rear suspension resulted in less-than-satisfactory roadholding and these cars had to be cornered with restraint. From 1965 onwards the main model was the 1300 with front-wheel drive and new and very stylish body. Its four-cylinder engine also powered the Spitfire sports car and the twin carburettor 75 bhp engine from this was installed in the 1300TC which appeared in 1967. There were many variations of these very successful cars, notably the 115-mph 1,998cc Dolomite with 16-valve overhead camshaft engine built in 1973–80 after the bodyshell had been re-engineered for rear-wheel drive.

The Herald, highly regarded at the time of its introduction, was not a landmark car like the Mini or the new Ford Anglia. Announced in August 1959, the Mini broke new ground and became an all-time classic design. Typed the ADO15, the original Mini was offered as the Austin Seven and the Morris Mini-Minor, but later became known simply as the Mini. By the time it appeared, front-wheel-drive was well-established, but Issigonis's ingenuity resulted in a car that was very different from anything offered by the opposition.

When the Mini first appeared, it had a BMC A-series engine of 848cc (63 × 68.26mm) with a power output of 34 bhp at 5,500 rpm and this was front-mounted transversely on a sub-frame with the four-speed gearbox mounted below the engine crankshaft and running in the engine sump. There was independent suspension front and rear, and rack-and-pinion steering. Although the Mini was only 10 feet long – 2 feet 4 inches shorter than the Morris Minor – the interior was roomier with more space for driver and passengers.

The earliest cars were very basic with features such as sliding windows and the doors opened and closed on the interior by a cable. At a price of £350 for the basic model (£496 19s. 2d with purchase tax) and the basic price of the de luxe version £28 10s. 0d extra, the Mini offered exceptional value for money, although the build-quality of early examples was poor. Maximum speed was 70 mph and fuel consumption bettered 45 mpg. Many changes were made to the Mini over the years and perhaps the most important was the adoption of Hydrolastic suspension in 1964, but this was not popular, and it did nothing for roadholding and general handling, although it softened the ride. It was abandoned in late 1969.

Above: The adoption, primarily from equestrian events, by the British Motor Corporation of the rosette as an identifying feature was neat and quite clever, and made the Corporation's products unmistakable.

More room in a small car

See for yourself how clever design has made full use of the room within the body of the Seven. The ten-inch wheels have been positioned as near as possible to the four extremities, which permits a wider-than-normal track, so taking up very little space inside the car. Each of the two front seats tips forward to give easier access to the wide rear seat. The driver's seat is adjustable on slides and in de luxe saloons the front passenger's seat can also be adjusted to suit its occupant. In a car of such modest dimensions it is a masterly achievement of styling that as much room—for head, legs and elbows I—has been provided within the Austin Seven as in many cars of much bigger exterior dimensions.

Introduced in 1959 in both Austin and Morris forms, this early Mini catalogue shows the Austin Seven version with the original very basic specification that included wire-pull door openers and sliding windows. Although the performance in standard form was not particularly impressive, the car's roadholding was superb.

Right: Much more sensible and practical than the Riley Elf and Wolseley Hornet (also Mini-based) were the Cooper high-performance versions of the Mini built from 1961 onwards. This is a standard 1965 998cc version photographed that year and fitted with the Moulton-design 'Hydrolastic' suspension with liquid damping that improved ride quality at the expense of handling. From 1969 the company began to abandon Hydrolastic suspension on Minis.

Above right: Although 'up-market' versions of the Mini and the 1100/1300 model sold in reasonable numbers – over 30,000 in the case of the Mini-based Riley Elf – this form of marketing debased once famous marques and did not add materially to sales. There is little doubt that the original buyer of this Riley Elf would, in other circumstances, have bought a Mini. This photograph shows an Elf III with 998cc engine, wind-up windows and all-synchromesh gearbox on the Spanish Island of Tenerife.

Already the Ford Popular had persuaded many motorcycle combination riders to switch from three wheels to four and the Mini reinforced the message. The Mini had a production life exceeding forty years and several million were built. Apart from the saloons and the Mini Cooper high-performance versions, there were estate cars, vans, pick-ups and, for some years, the jeep-style Moke. BMC also built versions with extended boot and superior trim as the Riley Elf and the Wolseley Hornet. The Mini set the agenda for future BMC popular car production and a whole range of front-wheel-drive cars followed.

The third of the trio of exciting family cars introduced in 1959 was Ford's new and very different version of the Anglia. Announced in September, the car proved a great success and between its introduction and 1967 over a million were sold (compared to over 1.5 million for the Mini in all its forms), with the major difference being that the Anglia made profits for Ford, while it was always argued (and cannot readily be challenged) that BMC never made any money out of the Mini. Why they could not remains one of the great mysteries of the British motor industry. Ford also continued production of the old 100E Anglia in stripped form as the Popular, and during the period 1959–62 built 126,000.

Powering the Anglia was a new four-cylinder 998cc engine with the over-square cylinder dimensions of 80.96×48.41mm and developing a very healthy 41 bhp. There was a unit construction chassis/body, MacPherson strut and coil spring independent front suspension and a rigid rear axle suspended on semi-elliptic leaf springs. The model was immediately recognisable by the reverse-slope rear window. It was a very fast small car with an 80 mph top speed, and it cornered well despite the rigid rear axle.

Left: It was not until 1959 that Ford of Great Britain introduced a really modern small car. It still retained the Anglia name and a rigid rear axle, but the power unit was an oversquare, very free-revving ohv unit and there was a four-speed gearbox. The reverse slope rear window made the new 105E Anglia instantly recognisable, and in eight years Ford sold well over a million examples.

The old Prefect with the new ohv engine remained in production until 1961 and in 1962 Ford introduced the Anglia Super with a 1,197cc longer-stroke version of the same engine.

Ford made a mistake with the Consul Classic of 1961–3 with American styling that was particularly poor: four hooded headlamps, reverse-slope rear window and high wing line leading into tail fins. The original engine size was 1,340cc, but it was increased to 1,498cc. Good points were the front disc brakes and the four-speed gearbox with floor change. Ford built around 110,000 of these cars and another 18,000 of the original Capri, a coupé version of the Classic.

In 1962 both BMC and Ford brought out important new models. From now on Ford was in the ascendancy because of the popularity of their Cortina and began to pull out an overall lead over BMC whose 1100 models were less popular. The Morris 1100 was an Issigonis front-wheel-drive design with

Left: Vauxhall executives at Luton gradually realised that the British market did not really want flamboyant, American-styled cars. In 1961 the company replaced the peculiar Victor F with the FB which was simpler in style and roomier. The first of these cars had the 1,508cc engine, but a 1,594cc unit was adopted in 1963.

comfortable seats for four and very neat well-balanced styling by Pininfarina (spelt as one word from 1961).

The Austin version followed a year later. Both had Hydrolastic suspension, disc front brakes, automatic transmission and, from 1967, the option of a 1,275cc engine, when they were called 1300 models. There were also versions offered with MG, Riley and Wolseley radiator grilles. The total production was in excess of 1.4 million between 1962 and 1973, but it has to be looked at in the light of what was happening at Dagenham, and it is difficult to equate production figures precisely because of differences in the model ranges.

Above: When the British Motor Corporation introduced the second of their front-wheel-drive cars, it was the 1100. Styling by Pininfarina was very sharp and well-balanced and the interior was exceptionally roomy. Hydrolastic suspension was fitted and these cars handled very well. This is an Austin version built in 1964.

Ford's Cortina was a conventional straightforward model with a simply styled four-door body (two-door versions were also available) and the choice of a 1,198cc or 1,498cc engine and a four-speed all-synchromesh gearbox. In simple terms the Cortina 1200 in 1963 had a basic price of £489 (£591 8s. 9d with purchase tax), while the Morris 1100 cost £490 basic (£592 12s. 11d). There was nothing to choose on price, but punters preferred Ford's traditional approach and in a four-year period 933,000 basic Cortinas were sold. In addition there were 77,000 of the GT model and 3,300 of the famed Lotus model.

During the 1960s Ford twice updated the larger-capacity models, with the Consul being replaced by the Zephyr 4. Dagenham added the Corsair, a model that fell between the Cortina and Zephyr in 1963. There was nothing special about these cars built in standard and 120GT 1,498cc forms. The GT was good for close to 95 mph and had its own special following. The company built 156,000 Corsairs with in-line engines before a new version appeared in 1965. This had a V4 1,663cc engine and there was also a Corsair GT with 1,996cc V4 engine and total production of both types of 135,000.

Right: Ford capitalised on the instant success of the Anglia and in 1962 introduced the first of the long line of top-selling Cortinas. The car shown here is a 1964 standard 1,198cc model. Ford had another million-plus seller in their stable and the company was winning the sales war with the British Motor Corporation.

Intended to slot in the range between the Cortina and the Zephyr, the Corsair had similar styling to the contemporary German Ford Taunus and an exceptionally good performance; the model stayed in production in various forms and sold in limited numbers for seven years.

In 1966 the Cortina II replaced the original model, the Escort superseded the Anglia and by the end of the decade Ford's conventional approach had won the hearts and minds of British motorists at the expense of the products of Cowley and Longbridge, where build standards had become poor, largely because of labour disputes. By the end of 1971 the whole range – with the exception of the Marina – had front-wheel drive.

The Rootes Group introduced a significant small family car when they launched the Imp, which was built in a new factory at Linwood in Scotland in 1963. The 845cc all-alloy single overhead camshaft engine was a development of the famous 1,098cc Coventry Climax engine that originated as the power unit for a portable fire pump and was a successful competition engine. Its success in sports cars encouraged Coventry Climax to develop the four-overhead-camshaft V8 engines that powered Jim Clark's World Championship Lotus cars in 1963 and 1965.

The Imp's engine was rear-mounted at a time when the leading Continental mass-manufacturers, VW and Renault, were contemplating switching to front engines and front-wheel drive. There was a quite delightful four-speed gearbox, the performance was superb and the economy excellent, but the handling was difficult to master. The biggest problem was that development of the new car had taken far too long and for financial reasons production had to start before the Imp was fully developed. There were many minor problems, some of which persisted for much of the Imp's production life, and the cars rusted away very rapidly.

Right: As the late
Michael Sedgwick
wrote about the
Ford Cortina, 'The
safe way's the
known way.' In
addition to the
two- and four-
door saloons, Ford
offered this
Cortina estate car
with faux wooden
strakes. Just how
many of this
particular version
were built is not
known.

Problems arising from the development costs of the Imp and its new factory necessitated the sale of a substantial stake in the Rootes Group to Chrysler in 1964 and a complete take-over in 1967. Apart from the standard Imp saloon, there was a vast number of variants that included Hillman Husky and Commer Cob (estate car and van), Singer Chamois saloon, Sunbeam Imp Sport saloon, Imp Californian, and Sunbeam Stiletto (coupés, as was the Chamois Sport).

Below: The
Rootes Group
continued to use
the Minx name for
its bigger Hillman
model. This is a
very stylish Super
Minx of 1965,
available with a
1,529cc or 1,725cc
engine, front disc
brakes and, in due
course, optional
Borg-Warner
automatic
transmission.

Unloved by the makers and most dealers, Imps lingered on in production to 1976. They were popular and successful in touring car events and some owners adored them. They had considerable charms to balance the defects, and in all their forms over half a million were produced. Chrysler decided to spend their money on a far more reactionary design and the result was the utterly conventional Cortina-inspired Avenger that appeared in 1970. Again, this was the sort of car that the British public really wanted, a point to which we shall return.

MEET THE **NEW**

HILLMAN IMP

AN INSPIRATION IN LIGHT CAR DESIGN

Both: Introduced in 1963, the Imp could have proved a saviour of the British motor industry if it had entered production fully sorted and without teething problems. The big, unanswerable question is whether the British public would have accepted a rear-engined car as the norm. This is a later car, c. 1969.

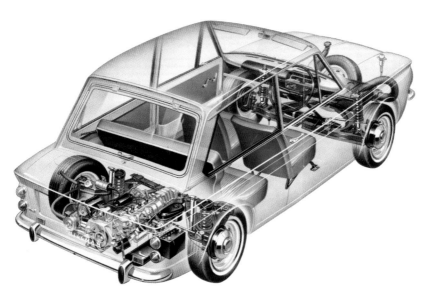

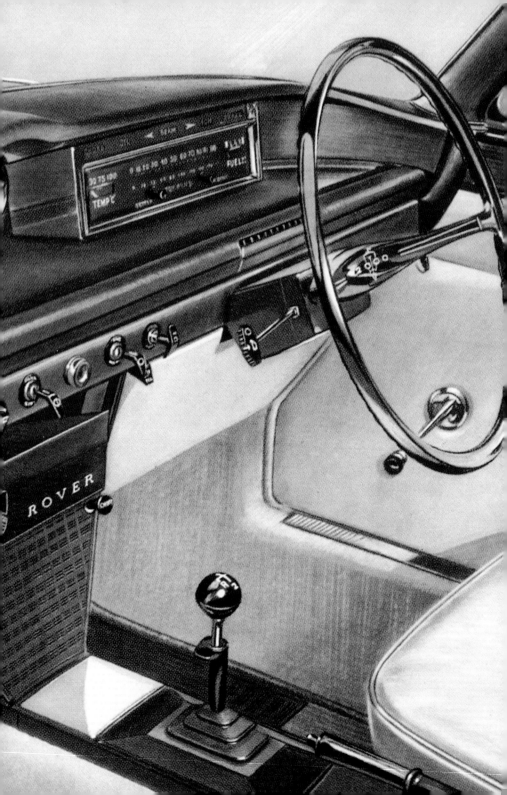

CARS FOR THE BETTER-OFF

ROVER AT Solihull became famed, and they still are, for the Land Rovers introduced in 1948, but the make's traditional place in the market was that of good quality, sober, restrained cars for the middle-class family and businessman. In early post-war days Rover, like most other British manufacturers, reintroduced pre-war models. For 1948 the company restricted its range to two models powered by ioe (that is overhead inlet and side exhaust valve) engines, the four-cylinder 1,595cc 60 (60 bhp) and the 2,103cc 75 (75 bhp). They were very traditional cars, as would be expected of Rover in the old days, but there was coil spring independent front suspension and a freewheel – a traditional Rover feature.

A year later Rover threw traditionalism overboard with a new 75 typed the P4 and later known as the Auntie. Motoring writer Ted Eves coined the name after a long and trouble-free journey across Europe in one, when he and his companions said that the car reminded them of the reliability of the clock on Auntie's mantelpiece. Yes, it was staid, but far less so than its predecessors, with slab-sided bodywork. The four-speed gearbox initially had the usual steering column change, although a floor-change was adopted on 1954 and later cars. The first cars had a Cyclops fog-lamp (abandoned in 1952), and hydraulic brakes were added from mid-1950. Over the years the basic concept was updated, with the four-cylinder 60 version reappearing (this time as a 2-litre) and the 90 with a 2,638cc engine introduced in 1953. These cars remained in production until 1964 and they were sadly missed when they were finally withdrawn.

In 1950 the first of the new 75s had a basic price of £865 (£1,106 0s. 7d with purchase tax) and by 1963 the 110 with 2,625cc engine, about to be phased out, was priced at £1,143 basic (£1,381 13s. 9d with purchase tax). A total of 130,000 of these cars of all types were built. By today's standards, they are rather ponderous and sluggish, but they were entirely British and all the better for it. A surprisingly high number of sometimes very rusty P4s are still used every day by their enthusiastic owners.

This was not the end of the traditional Rover, for the Solihull company introduced its P5 3-litre car in 1958; it was a big platform-style car widely

Opposite:
Introduced in 1963, the Rover 2000 was superbly styled with Italianate looks, and was subsequently available both in twin-carburettor form and with the Buick-derived 3,528cc V8 engine. The only problem was that the mergers that led to British Leyland resulted in two top of the range, exceptionally high-quality saloons competing with one other. The other car was of course the Triumph 2000/2500.

Above: Rover introduced the P4 75 with 2,103cc engine at the 1949 London Show. It was a fine solid car that appealed to the upper-middle-class family motorist. Early cars had the single Cyclops fog-lamp set in the centre of the grille. This is a 1955 example and from the autumn of that year the 75 had a new short-stroke engine. In addition to the 2,230cc 75, Land Rover offered the 60 with a four-cylinder 1,997cc Land Rover engine, and the higher-performance 90 with a 2,639cc six-cylinder engine.

Above: Introduced in 1963, the Rover 2000 was superbly styled with Italianate looks, and was subsequently available both in twin-carburettor form and with the Buick-derived 3,528cc V8 engine. The only problem was that the mergers that led to British Leyland resulted in two top-of-the-range, exceptionally high-quality saloons competing with one other. The other car was of course the Triumph 2000/2500.

used by government officials and in the North of England as a family car by mill owners, a dying breed. From 1962, a low-roof four-door Coupé joined the saloon, and from 1967 both models were re-equipped with the ex-Buick V8 3,528cc engine. Now called 3.5-litres, they had a 112mph top speed.

Rover introduced the very nicely styled four-cylinder P6 2000 series in 1963 and these exceptionally attractive cars, also available as TC (Twin Carburettor) and with the 3.5-litre V8 engine as the automatic 3500 and the manual 3500S, were in production well into the 1970s. Rover enlarged the four-cylinder engine to make a 2200 from 1973 to 1976. Exact production figures are in dispute, but around 327,000 of all types were built, of which around 79,000 had the V8 engine.

By this time Rover was part of British Leyland, as was Triumph, who made a car that competed directly with this Rover model. This was the very good six-cylinder 2000 and the exceptionally good 2500 built in saloon and estate car versions from the late 1960s. The 2500 MK II was available until 1975. The carburettor version developed 106 bhp, had overdrive as standard and a maximum speed of 100 mph. This was a quite brilliant car and a delight to drive even under modern day road conditions.

It was preceded by the 2.5 PI with Lucas fuel injection, which was never properly sorted and how well it ran depended on barometric pressure. It could be fine in the valley but if you took it up to the summit of a hill it might start to run roughly. Total production of the 2000 and 2500 Triumphs amounted to 275,000 and again it must be stressed that these production figures are indicative rather than precise. A direct comparison with Rover on price is possible: in 1963 the new Rover 2000 cost £1,046 (£1,264 9s. 7d) and the equivalent Triumph was priced at £905 (£1094 2s. 0d with purchase tax).

One of the more innovative of post-war family cars was the Jowett Javelin, built at Idle near Bradford. They went well and handled well, but the company failed in 1953 because it could not sell enough to use the bodies that Briggs had contracted to supply from their Doncaster factory. As a result there was a large stock of Javelins, and new cars could still be bought for some while.

An almost-forgotten name is Jowett, who were in business for a very long time at Idle near Bradford building modest little cars with horizontally opposed twin and four-cylinder engines. This all changed in post-war days with the Javelin, very much a 'middle of the road' family tourer, but with sporting pretensions. The Javelin retained a horizontally opposed four-cylinder engine, which was mounted ahead of the radiator. The specification included independent torsion bar suspension at the front, rack-and-pinion steering and 80 mph-plus performance. There was a four-speed steering-column gear-change, but even this was quite tolerable compared with the majority of its type.

The Javelin first appeared in 1947 and in the early days there were engine problems which were not fully resolved until 1952. Although 23,000 of these cars were built, the problems had caused a loss of confidence and the company could not sell cars quickly enough to consume the flow of bodies that Briggs were contracted to supply from their Doncaster factory. A receiver was appointed and production of Javelins ceased, together with the Jupiter sports and the incredibly successful Bradford flat-twin van and estate car (38,000 sold).

Lord Nuffield's organisation had since pre-war days built up-market family cars, MGs and Rileys, both assembled at Cowley. MG's early post-war saloons were the 1,250cc YA and YB (there were only minor differences between the two) built between 1947 and 1953. A small number of YT Tourers were also constructed in 1948–50. In 1953 MG introduced the very attractive ZA Magnette saloon, which had great character despite sharing its unit-construction body/chassis with the 1,250cc Wolseley 4/44 and using the 1,489cc BMC B-series engine.

Although the drive was conventional – to the rear wheels – the horizontally opposed four-cylinder engine of the Javelin was mounted well to the front of the car to maintain good weight distribution.

The ZA went well, handled well, braked well and it had good trim quality and a high level of comfort. After 18,000 had been produced, MG introduced the ZB with its more powerful 64 bhp engine, Varitone two-tone paint finish and a wrap-round rear window. It was still a great car, but the image of MG saloons was to be lost in the horrors of BMC badge-engineering and Pinin Farina's styling.

Nuffield had bought Riley when that company was in severe financial difficulties in 1938. It was a marque with a great history and although some diehard enthusiasts claim the marque lost its character, many would argue that the post-war 1½-litre RMA/RME (1946–55 – 14,000 built) and the 2½-litre RMB and RMF (1946–53 – 8,000 built) were great cars. They were powered by the traditional four-cylinder Riley engines with pushrod ohvs operated by twin camshafts mounted high on the block. The 2½-litre cars developed 100 bhp (from 1948), had a 90 mph performance, superb, sleek greyhound lines and good build-quality.

They were not cheap, and in their last years the RMFs were priced at £1,055 (£1,642 5s. 2d with purchase tax). There were also a small number of drophead coupés. The replacement for the RMF was the Pathfinder, with slab-sided, but roomy body as used for the Wolseley 6/90 and retaining the original Riley 2½-litre engine. For 1958 it was replaced by the 2.6 with the BMC C-series engine and, radiator grille apart, was identical to the Wolseley 6/90. Another great marque had bitten the dust.

One of the most significant and prestigious post-war British marques was Jaguar. Although this Coventry company built outstanding sports cars, its main product was fast, comfortable and well-equipped touring cars that were sold at comparatively modest prices. All were powered by versions of the famed twin-overhead-camshaft XK engine. That they were family cars is

The post-war Riley 2½-litre saloon with sleek, sporting lines and a maximum speed of around 90 mph was a magnificent fast touring car with plenty of space for four adults. It was the best car built by the Nuffield Organisation. This 1952 example is competing in the 1954 Lancia Motor Club Rally.

undoubted, and they were very popular with the well-heeled middle-class who lived in expensive middle-class areas. Sometimes, they were chauffeur-driven, just as sometimes were Rovers and the Sunbeam-Talbot sporting saloons built by the Rootes group.

Sunbeam-Talbot was a combination of two marque names in pre-war days that were acquired by the Rootes Group. The 90 had a 2,267cc engine as used in the Humber Hawk and the model was superbly styled by American Raymond Lowey's design office. The family who ran this 1951 car bought it in 1958 in preference to running a small Ford or Austin.

RETROSPECTION

D URING THE 1960s the British motor industry had made valiant efforts to overcome the complacency that had set in immediately after the Second World War. This had resulted from a vast demand for cars, regardless of their technical competence, in Britain and export markets, especially the old British Empire. There was, initially, little opposition, as American cars were so big, bulky and expensive to run and because of the ravages of the war the manufacturers on the European mainland were not ready to do more than satisfy local demand.

This all changed; MG pioneered the sale of sports cars in the United States and although British touring cars were in the main unwanted by North American buyers, Austin-Healey, Triumph and Jaguar, along with other British sports car manufacturers, developed a niche market and a faithful customer base. The one European touring car that sold in large numbers in the United States was the VW and for many years the Wolfsburg company had difficulty in meeting demand.

By 1970, the end of the era that has been discussed, the British motor industry was mortally wounded. Because so many British manufacturers had become uncompetitive, they merged and the ultimate disaster was British Leyland, formed in 1968. The vast number of marques within the group included Austin, MG, Morris, Riley, Wolseley, Jaguar, Daimler, Rover, Standard and Triumph. Only to a very limited extent did these marques compete with each other, but the group as a whole gradually lost market share.

The companies in the British Leyland group that came from the British Motor Corporation had very effectively managed their own downfall. Industrial relations were abysmal and the group was riddled with disputes and strikes. Build quality was quite simply conspicuous by its absence and cars were delivered rusty and defective. Many potential buyers were also deterred by the Group's badge-engineering whereby there were as many as five or six versions of the same model distinguishable only by the radiator grille and the name on the badge.

Another problem faced by this division was that it had pinned its prospects of success almost completely on the front-wheel-drive designs of Alec Issigonis. BMC were pioneers of the mass production of front-wheel-drive cars, but they were premature and the market was to show that more motorists preferred the basic, simple designs built by Ford and Vauxhall. The Triumph division of British Leyland arguably built the best family cars on the British market, but Triumph was a poor relation of the group that was never sufficiently promoted and developed.

In addition the British manufacturers faced serious and rapidly growing opposition from the Japanese, who did not market cars in Britain until the 1960s. Increasingly, the choice lay between the British-built cars (Ford and Vauxhall) or the Japanese Nissan (originally Datsun) and Toyota. These Japanese cars were initially difficult to sell because there were too many memories of Japanese atrocities in the Second World War, but younger generations have shorter memories and less prejudice. That the Japanese cars were very traditional in concept, sturdily constructed and well built stood in their favour, together with very low initial purchase prices.

As the 1960s closed and British Leyland was beginning to struggle, very few people seriously realised that the motoring world was destined to change. There was no inkling then that production would cease at both the Ford plant at Dagenham and the Vauxhall factory at Luton. There was no suspicion that Rover (as British Leyland became known in 1986) would have to be rescued by the government and after passing through various ownerships would finally collapse in 2005.

No-one would have supposed that Toyota would become the world's biggest and most profitable manufacturer, while both Ford and General Motors in the United States would struggle to survive. With the current global rise in fuel prices, a booming Chinese economy and increasing concerns about the environment, there are serious moral questions relating to the motor car and the need to make more use of public transport.

Farina's designs for the British Motor Corporation always looked better in illustrations than in the metal. At the time they were built, cars such as this Morris Oxford were criticised for their silly tail fins, the angular lines and the large areas of blank sheet metal, but – with the benefit of hindsight – this car looks good, apart from disproportionally small wheels.

SUGGESTED READING

Georgano, G. N. (Editor). *The Complete Encyclopaedia of Motorcars 1885 to the Present*. Second Edition, Ebury Press, 1973.

Hopfinger, K. B. *Beyond Expectation, The Volkswagen Story*. G. T. Foulis, 1954.

Langworth, Richard. *Tiger, Alpine, Rapier, Sporting Cars from the Rootes Group*. Osprey Publishing, 1982.

Langworth, Richard, and Robson, Graham. *Triumph Cars, The Complete 75-Year History*. Motor Racing Publications, 1979.

Olyslager, P. N. *Motor Manuals* (Most British cars of the 1960s and 1970s). Thomas Nelson, various dates.

Pomeroy, Lawrence. *The Mini Story*. Temple Press, 1964.

Robson, Graham. *Mini*. (Haynes Great Car Series), Haynes Publishing, 2006.

Rolt, L. T. C. *Motoring History*. Dutton Vista, 1964.

Skilleter, Paul. *The Morris Minor*. Osprey Publishing, 1981.

Wyatt, R. J., *The Austin Motor Car*, David & Charles, 1968.

PLACES TO VISIT

Coventry Transport Museum, Millenium Square, Hales Street, Coventry. Website: www.transport-museum.com. A superb display of Coventry–built cars, commercial vehicles and buses with just about every relevant make represented, and all of them displayed in an intelligent and attractive manner.

Heritage Motor Centre, Gaydon, Warwickshire (just off the M40). Website: www.heritage-motor-centre.co.uk Originally devoted to vehicles of the constituent companies of what became the Rover Group, Alvis, Austin, MG, Morris, Standard, Triumph, Wolseley, etc., the scope of vehicles exhibited was extended after the Ford acquisition of Land Rover some years ago.

National Motor Museum, Palace House, Beaulieu, Hampshire. Website: www.beaulieu.co.uk An older museum with an excellent collection of vehicles, but not always presented in the best manner. Apart from touring cars, the exhibits include Land Speed Record cars and an ex-works team car 1923/4 Grand Prix Sunbeam.

INDEX